THE GOLDEN STORE

Contents

Foreword

by Jack Mapanje

I have admired and enjoyed the poetry of William Wordsworth since I was young. I was born on the banks of the third largest lake in Africa, surrounded by mountain ranges, smaller lakes or waters and numerous rivers – most of which had crocodiles! Perfect environment for one's relish of Wordsworth's nature and landscape poetry! And while I have been a poet-in-residence at the Wordsworth Trust, Dove Cottage, for the past two years, my understanding and appreciation of his poetry has deepened. I have run creative writing workshops at Dove Cottage and in schools around the Lake District and beyond, often by using Wordsworth's poetry and emphasising the relevance, timelessness and global nature of its content and form.

I find Nancy Martin's selection particularly welcome as it encapsulates William Wordsworth as a boy and as a man. Her illustrations capture the mood and tone of the poems perfectly. The notes that accompany what might be considered rather difficult poems, and her explanation of difficult words, concepts and forms, help to make the poems more accessible. What makes Wordsworth's poetry appealing throughout the world, more than one hundred and fifty years on, is its subject matter, which has been clearly divided and indicated in this selection.

William Wordsworth reacted to, wrote and read about what the ordinary person today reacts to and would want to write or read about. We play or hang out with our mates at night or during the day. We are excited about the hustle and bustle of city life; we go fishing; we visit far off places; we are affected by the weather; we talk about love – these are some of the subjects which inspired the poet. And like most writers who mirror their age, William Wordsworth also reacted to the political affairs of his time. The poem 'September 1st, 1802' (and others) shows Wordsworth's disgust with the injustices of the world –

in this case with Napoleon Bonaparte's decree that all Negroes should be thrown out of France, even after the official abolition of the slave trade and slavery. How relevant to issues of race and asylum could a writer be!

Go on, turn the pages of *The Golden Store* and enjoy the poems.

Jack Mapanje was born in 1944 in Malawi, Africa. Now living in Britain, he has published numerous collections of poems. Jack is a human rights activist. Some of his poems describe his experiences when his writing was banned by the Malawi government and he was imprisoned without charge or trial for nearly four years. He now teaches in the School of English at the University of Newcastle upon Tyne.

Introduction

And afterwards, when, to my father's house
Returning at the holidays, I found
That golden store of books which I had left
Open to my enjoyment once again,
What heart was mine!

Since his death over a hundred and fifty years ago, William Wordsworth's poems have become increasingly popular and well-loved. His work is now seen as 'classic' poetry. If you are not used to reading classic poetry, it may be that you are not quite sure what to expect, especially if it has 'old-fashioned' language. This collection however, is full of ways to help you enjoy and understand the poems. The illustrations are there to set the scene for the poetry and give you an idea of what each poem is about, while easy information and explanations fill in what you might want to know.

The collection is divided into six sections, each of which looks at a different topic. It also has many extracts from longer poems. These have been given 'new' titles so they appear like poems in their own right. The index at the back provides details about all the poems and where the extracts come from. If you enjoy the extracts, you may well want to read the full poems in the future.

Three of the sections contain extracts from the journals written by Wordsworth's sister Dorothy. As well as recording her daily life, Dorothy filled her journals with descriptions of the world around her. She once commented that nature could inspire her to be 'more than half a poet': you will find that these short pieces capture your imagination rather like a poem.

The collection is named after Wordsworth's 'golden store' of books that he read as a boy. They were, he said, 'open to my enjoyment'. Now it is your turn to open his poems and enjoy them.

William Wordsworth's life

1770
William Wordsworth is born on 7 April in Cockermouth,
Cumbria, the second of five children. His mother Ann dies
when he is eight and, five years later in 1783 his father John,
a lawyer, dies. Wordsworth has lost both parents by the age
of thirteen, but has become particularly close to his only
sister, Dorothy.

1776–7
He attends Ann Birkett's infant school in Penrith.

1779
He is sent to Hawkshead Grammar School, boarding out in
the village with a lady named Ann Tyson.

1787
He goes to Cambridge University.

1791–2
He spends most of this period in France.

1795
He moves to Dorset with his sister Dorothy and begins to
concentrate on writing poetry.

1797– 8
He and Dorothy live in Somerset near their friend, Samuel
Taylor Coleridge, another poet. Wordsworth writes many
poems and Dorothy starts keeping her journal.

1799
He moves back to Cumbria with Dorothy, settling at Dove
Cottage, Grasmere. During the next eight years at the cottage,
he writes many of his most popular poems.

1802
He marries Mary Hutchinson. Dorothy continues to live with
them.

1803

Birth of William and Mary's son John. Other children born over the next seven years are Dora (1804), Thomas (1806), Catherine (1808) and William (1810).

1805

William and Dorothy's lives are hit by tragedy when their brother John, a sailor, is among over two hundred people drowned in a shipwreck.

1808

The Wordsworth family leave Dove Cottage and move to a new house in Grasmere, Allan Bank.

1811

The family moves to The Rectory, next to St. Oswald's church in Grasmere.

1812

Two of William and Mary's children die. Catherine (three) dies of a fit and Thomas (six) dies as a result of catching measles.

1813

The Wordsworths move to Rydal Mount, a large house two miles from Grasmere. During his thirty-seven years here, his poetry achieves wide popularity and he becomes increasingly famous.

1843

He is appointed Poet Laureate to Queen Victoria. Although he is expected to write poems about royal events, Wordsworth is the only Poet Laureate in British history to write no official poetry at all.

1850

23 April: William Wordsworth dies and is buried in Grasmere churchyard. Dorothy dies nearly five years later. Her grave is near Wordsworth's.

'Spots of Time'

Special Moments from a Lake District Childhood

Like all of us, Wordsworth never forgot certain things that happened when he was a boy. The happiest or most exciting moments were the ones he remembered best but the most frightening, troubling or saddest times also remained vividly in his mind. He called all these special memories 'spots of time'. Not surprisingly, the Lake District landscape was an important feature in them.

Wordsworth's 'spots of time' were particularly precious for him because they were often moments that fired his imagination – and for someone who wanted to be a poet, that was important.

All of us have our own 'spots of time'. If you think back over your own life, you probably cannot remember what you had for dinner this time last week, but there will be certain events or experiences you know you will never forget.

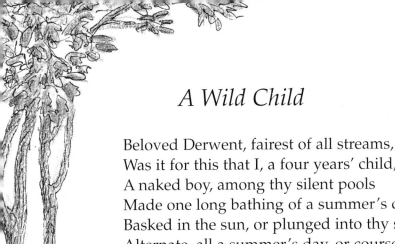

A Wild Child

Beloved Derwent, fairest of all streams,
Was it for this that I, a four years' child,
A naked boy, among thy silent pools
Made one long bathing of a summer's day,
Basked in the sun, or plunged into thy streams,
Alternate, all a summer's day, or coursed
Over the sandy fields, and dashed the flowers
Of yellow grunsel; or, when crag and hill,
The woods, and distant Skiddaw's lofty height,
Were bronzed with a deep radiance, stood alone
A naked savage in the thunder-shower?

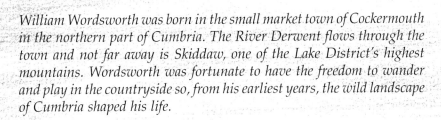

William Wordsworth was born in the small market town of Cockermouth
in the northern part of Cumbria. The River Derwent flows through the
town and not far away is Skiddaw, one of the Lake District's highest
mountains. Wordsworth was fortunate to have the freedom to wander
and play in the countryside so, from his earliest years, the wild landscape
of Cumbria shaped his life.

'coursed': ran   'grunsel' or groundsel: a common wild flower

The Drowned Man

Twilight was coming on, yet through the gloom
I saw distinctly on the opposite shore,
Beneath a tree and close by the lake side,
A heap of garments, as if left by one
Who there was bathing. Half an hour I watched
And no one owned them; meanwhile the calm lake
Grew dark with all the shadows on its breast,
And now and then a leaping fish disturbed
The breathless stillness. The succeeding day
There came a company, and in their boat
Sounded with iron hooks and with long poles.
At length the dead man, 'mid that beauteous scene
Of trees and hills and water, bolt upright
Rose with his ghastly face.

When he was eight, Wordsworth's mother died. The following year he was sent to school in Hawkshead about forty miles away where, during term-time, he lodged with a local woman, Ann Tyson. He had only been there a short time when he witnessed a tragedy on nearby Esthwaite Water. James Jackson, a local teacher, drowned while bathing in the lake and his body was discovered by men who 'sounded' or dragged the water with hooks and poles.

4

Summer in Hawkshead

                    Duly were our games
Prolonged in summer till the daylight failed:
No chair remained before the doors, the bench
And threshold steps were empty, fast asleep
The labourer and the old man who had sat
A later lingerer, yet the revelry
Continued and the loud uproar. At last,
When all the ground was dark and the huge clouds
Were edged with twinkling stars, to bed we went
With weary joints and with a beating mind.

Wordsworth enjoyed his time at Hawkshead School and made some good friends. On summer evenings they played around the village long after everyone else was indoors.

'threshold steps': front door steps
'lingerer': to 'linger' is to delay or hang around

A Summer Day at Windermere

Upon the eastern shore of Windermere
Above the crescent of a pleasant bay
There was an inn … The garden lay
Upon a slope surmounted by the plain
Of a small bowling-green; beneath us stood
A grove, with gleams of water through the trees
And over the tree-tops – nor did we want
Refreshment, strawberries and mellow cream –
And there through half an afternoon we played
On the smooth platform, and the shouts we sent
Made all the mountains ring.

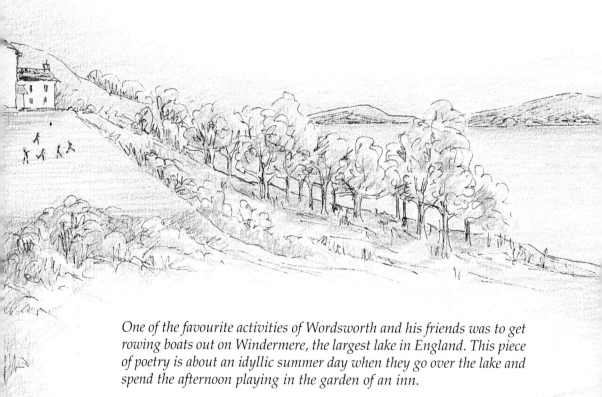

One of the favourite activities of Wordsworth and his friends was to get rowing boats out on Windermere, the largest lake in England. This piece of poetry is about an idyllic summer day when they go over the lake and spend the afternoon playing in the garden of an inn.

But ere the fall
Of night, when in our pinnace we returned
Over the dusky lake, and to the beach
Of some small island steered our course, with one,
The minstrel of our troop, and left him there,
And rowed off gently, while he blew his flute
Alone upon the rock, oh, then the calm
And dead still water lay upon my mind
Even with a weight of pleasure, and the sky,
Never before so beautiful, sank down
Into my heart and held me like a dream.

As the sun begins to set, they row back across the lake but on the way they land on one of its many small islands. The 'minstrel of the troop' (the musician of their little group, a lad called Robert Greenwood) plays his flute while the others drift around on the water.

alien sounds

melancholy

precipices
rang
aloud

solitary cliffs wheeled by

icy
crags
tinkled
like
iron

shadowy banks came sweeping through the darkness

spinning

games confederate

tumult

imitative of the chase

polished ice

wheeled about
like an untired horse

tranqui
as a
summ
sea

flew

proud and exulting

hissing

shod with steel

Winter in Hawkshead

And in the frosty season, when the sun
Was set, and visible for many a mile
The cottage windows through the twilight blazed,
I heeded not the summons. Clear and loud
The village clock tolled six; I wheeled about
Proud and exulting, like an untired horse
That cares not for its home. All shod with steel
We hissed along the polished ice in games
Confederate, imitative of the chase
And woodland pleasures, the resounding horn,
The pack loud bellowing, and the hunted hare.
So through the darkness and the cold we flew,
And not a voice was idle. With the din,
Meanwhile, the precipices rang aloud;
The leafless trees and every icy crag
Tinkled like iron; while the distant hills
Into the tumult sent an alien sound
Of melancholy, not unnoticed; while the stars,
Eastward, were sparkling clear, and in the west
The orange sky of evening died away.

One of the highlights of winter in Hawkshead was ice-skating on Esthwaite Water. Wordsworth and his friends liked to join in the fun, sometimes skating in the evenings, probably after school. Imagine what that might have been like – dark, cold, exciting, dangerous ...

In this piece of poetry, Wordsworth describes how the hills and cliffs ('precipices') echo to the sound of shouts and laughter as he and his friends join together to play games ('games confederate'). Their noise, or 'tumult', and the way they rush around remind him of a hunt, with dogs barking and the huntsman blowing his horn.

Not seldom from the uproar I retired
Into a silent bay, or sportively
Glanced sideway, leaving the tumultuous throng,
To cut across the shadow of a star
That gleamed upon the ice. And oftentimes
When we had given our bodies to the wind,
And all the shadowy banks on either side
Came sweeping through the darkness, spinning still
The rapid line of motion, then at once
Have I, reclining back upon my heels
Stopped short – yet still the solitary cliffs
Wheeled by me, even as if the earth had rolled
With visible motion her diurnal round.
Behind me did they stretch in solemn train,
Feebler and feebler, and I stood and watched
Till all was tranquil as a summer sea.

*Skating on his own into a quieter area, Wordsworth whirls around. When
he stops suddenly, he feels dizzy and has the sensation that the earth is still
spinning round him. Gradually the feeling wears off (it gets 'feebler and
feebler') and everything is 'tranquil' – calm and peaceful – once more.*

Winter Evenings

We were a noisy crew; the sun in heaven
Beheld not vales more beautiful than ours,
Nor saw a race in happiness and joy
More worthy of the fields where they were sown.
I would record with no reluctant voice
Our home amusements by the warm peat fire
At evening, when with pencil and with slate,
In square divisions parcelled out, and all
With crosses and with cyphers scribbled o'er,
We schemed and puzzled, head opposed to head,
In strife too humble to be named in verse …
                    Meanwhile abroad
The heavy rain was falling, or the frost
Raged bitterly with keen and silent tooth,
And, interrupting the impassioned game,
Oft from the neighbouring lake the splitting ice,
While it sank down towards the water, sent
Among the meadows and the hills its long
And frequent yellings, imitative some
Of wolves that howl along the Bothnic main.

If they could not be outside, Wordsworth and his friends liked to gather by the fireside to play card games and noughts and crosses, using slates to write on. When Esthwaite Water was frozen, they sometimes interrupted their games to listen to the sound of the ice. As it moved and broke apart it seemed to Wordsworth that the eerie noise was like the howling of wolves. The 'Bothnic main' is part of Russia, where wolves are found.

the sky seemed not a sky of earth

strange utterance

perilous ridge

half-inch fissures

I hung alone

knots of grass

shouldering the naked crag

loud dry wind blows through my ears

suspended by the blast which blew amain

ill sustained

raven's nest

slippery rock

The Raven's Nest

Nor less in springtime, when on southern banks
The shining sun had from his knot of leaves
Decoyed the primrose flower, and when the vales
And woods were warm, was I a rover then
In the high places, on the lonesome peaks,
Among the mountains and the winds …
                        Oh, when I have hung
Above the raven's nest, by knots of grass
Or half-inch fissures in the slippery rock
But ill-sustained, and almost, as it seemed,
Suspended by the blast which blew amain,
Shouldering the naked crag, oh, at that time,
While on the perilous ridge I hung alone,
With what strange utterance did the loud dry wind
Blow through my ears; the sky seemed not a sky
Of earth, and with what motion moved the clouds!

More than anything, Wordsworth liked to roam among the lakes and mountains alone. Sometimes he got himself into dangerous or frightening situations and he began to understand just how powerful the forces of nature could be. In this piece of poetry, he scrambles over a cliff edge ('perilous ridge') trying to reach a bird's nest. Clinging on by his fingertips, he feels that the strength of the wind is keeping him up – as if he is 'suspended by the blast'.

'fissure': a long, narrow crack in the rock
'ill-sustained': badly supported   'amain': stormy, violent

Owl Calls

There was a boy – ye knew him well, ye cliffs
And islands of Winander – many a time
At evening, when the stars had just begun
To move along the edges of the hills,
Rising or setting, would he stand alone
Beneath the trees or by the glimmering lake,
And there, with fingers interwoven, both hands
Pressed closely palm to palm, and to his mouth
Uplifted, he as through an instrument
Blew mimic hootings to the silent owls
That they might answer him. And they would shout
Across the watery vale, and shout again,
Responsive to his call, with quivering peals
And long halloos, and screams, and echoes loud,
Redoubled and redoubled – concourse wild
Of mirth and jocund din.

The young Wordsworth soon began to develop a passionate love of nature. In this piece of poetry, he describes a boy (who is really himself) blowing through his hands to make owl calls, in the hope of getting real owls to answer. The lake is Windermere (Winander).

Waiting for Horses

One Christmas-time,
The day before the holidays began,
Feverish, and tired, and restless, I went forth
Into the fields, impatient for the sight
Of those three horses which should bear us home,
My brothers and myself. There was a crag,
An eminence, which from the meeting-point
Of two highways ascending overlooked
At least a long half-mile of those two roads,
By each of which the expected steeds might come –
The choice uncertain. Thither I repaired
Up to the highest summit. 'Twas a day
Stormy, and rough, and wild, and on the grass
I sat half sheltered by a naked wall.
Upon my right hand was a single sheep,
A whistling hawthorn on my left, and there,
Those two companions at my side, I watched
With eyes intensely straining, as the mist
Gave intermitting prospects of the wood
And plain beneath. Ere I to school returned
That dreary time, ere I had been ten days
A dweller in my father's house, he died,
And I and my two brothers, orphans then,
Followed his body to the grave.

When Wordsworth was thirteen, his father died suddenly. He had become
ill after spending a stormy night out in the open as the result of getting
lost on the bleak and lonely moor of Cold Fell near Egremont in west
Cumbria. Here, Wordsworth recalls waiting impatiently for the arrival of
horses ('steeds') that have been hired to take him and his brothers home
for Christmas. Although he does not yet know that his father is seriously
ill, the wild and gloomy landscape seems to set the scene for the tragedy
to come.

'eminence': a high view-point   'ere': before

Stealing a Boat

                    … one evening …
I went alone into a shepherd's boat,
A skiff, that to a willow-tree was tied
Within a rocky cave, its usual home.
The moon was up, the lake was shining clear
Among the hoary mountains; from the shore
I pushed, and struck the oars, and struck again
In cadence, and my little boat moved on
Just like a man who walks with stately step
Though bent on speed. It was an act of stealth
And troubled pleasure.

By the time he was in his teens, Wordsworth knew he had a good imagination but it took a strange experience to convince him just how powerful it was. It begins when he discovers a boat (he also calls it a 'skiff', a 'bark' or a 'pinnace') on a lake shore. Foolishly, he decides to take it and row onto the lake in the dark. He describes his feelings as 'troubled pleasure' – he has a mixture of guilt and excitement.

                    Not without the voice
Of mountain echoes did my boat move on,
Leaving behind her still on either side
Small circles glittering idly in the moon,
Until they melted all into one track
Of sparkling light. A rocky steep uprose
Above the cavern of the willow-tree,
And now, as suited one who proudly rowed
With his best skill, I fixed a steady view
Upon the top of that same craggy ridge,
The bound of the horizon – for behind
Was nothing but the stars and the grey sky.

Enjoying the motion of the boat on the moonlit water and proud of his skill in rowing, Wordsworth concentrates his gaze on the highest point he can see ('the bound of the horizon').

She was an elfin pinnace; twenty times
I dipped my oars into the silent lake,
And as I rose upon the stroke my boat
Went heaving through the water like a swan –
When from behind that rocky steep, till then
The bound of the horizon, a huge cliff,
As if with voluntary power instinct,
Upreared its head. I struck, and struck again,
And, growing still in stature, the huge cliff
Rose up between me and the stars, and still,
With measured motion, like a living thing
Strode after me. With trembling hands I turned,
And through the silent water stole my way
Back to the cavern of the willow-tree.

Without warning, another much higher mountain rears up into Wordsworth's view. He suddenly becomes terrified and imagines that it is following him with a power all of its own ('voluntary power instinct'). Trembling with fear, he steals his way back to the shore to return the boat.

There in her mooring-place I left my bark,
And through the meadows homeward went with grave
And serious thoughts; and after I had seen
That spectacle, for many days my brain
Worked with a dim and undetermined sense
Of unknown modes of being. In my thoughts
There was a darkness – call it solitude,
Or blank desertion – no familiar shapes
Of hourly objects, images of trees,
Of sea or sky, no colours of green fields,
But huge and mighty forms that do not live
Like living men moved slowly through my mind
By day, and were the trouble of my dreams.

Although Wordsworth knows that his fear is all imagined, he is very unsettled by the whole experience. He turns it over and over in his mind, trying to make sense of it. However, the images continue to haunt him, dominating his life and affecting his normal ways of thinking. Even the familiar world of nature, which normally gives him so much pleasure, takes on a menacing, unreal character.

A Golden Store of Books

And afterwards, when, to my father's house
Returning at the holidays, I found
That golden store of books which I had left
Open to my enjoyment once again,
What heart was mine! Full often through the course
Of those glad respites in the summertime
When armed with rod and line we went abroad
For a whole day together, I have lain
Down by thy side, O Derwent, murmuring stream,
On the hot stones and in the glaring sun,
And there have read, devouring as I read,
Defrauding the day's glory – desperate –
Till with a sudden bound of smart reproach
Such as an idler deals with in his shame,
I to my sport betook myself again.

As far back as he could remember, Wordsworth loved books and what he called 'the mystery of words'. He read anything he could lay his hands on, although there was not the wide choice we have nowadays – no Harry Potter in the eighteenth century! He delighted in traditional folk tales, adventures, legends, romances, fairy stories, travel books – and of course, poetry. In this piece of poetry, he even admits to taking a book with him when he went fishing.

London

*William Wordsworth first visited London at the age of
eighteen. He had never been to a large city before and the
small market towns of Cumbria hardly prepared him for the
vast crowds and bustle of London. As well as writing about
his impressions of hectic city life, he also described the quieter,
more peaceful times when hardly anyone was about.*

*Wordsworth's poem about crossing Westminster Bridge was
written when he was thirty-two. He was with Dorothy at the
time and you can imagine their excitement at seeing London
on such a beautiful morning.*

Images of London

Traffic

The endless stream of men and moving things …
The wealth, the bustle and the eagerness,
The glittering chariots with their pampered steeds,
Stalls, barrows, porters, midway in the street
The scavenger that begs with hat in hand,
The labouring hackney-coaches, the rash speed
Of coaches travelling far, whirled on with horn
Loud blowing …

Shops

Here, there, and everywhere, a weary throng,
The comers and the goers face to face –
Face after face – the string of dazzling wares,
Shop after shop …

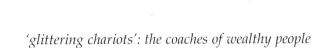

'glittering chariots': the coaches of wealthy people
'scavenger': a beggar
'hackney-coaches': the first taxis

23

Crowds

Above all, one thought
Baffled my understanding, how men lived
Even next-door neighbours, as we say, yet still
Strangers, and knowing not each other's names …

How often in the overflowing streets
Have I gone forwards with the crowd, and said
Unto myself, 'The face of every one
That passes by me is a mystery.'

Night-time

        … the peace
Of night, for instance …
When the great tide of human life stands still,
The business of the day to come unborn,
Of that gone by locked up as in the grave;
The calmness, beauty, of the spectacle,
Sky, stillness, moonshine, empty streets, and sounds
Unfrequent as in deserts; at late hours
Of winter evenings when unwholesome rains
Are falling hard, with people yet astir,
The feeble salutation from the voice
Of some unhappy woman now and then
Heard as we pass, when no one looks about,
Nothing is listened to.

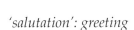

'salutation': greeting

St Paul's Cathedral in the snow

      … a length of street
Laid open in its morning quietness,
Deep, hollow, unobstructed, vacant, smooth,
And white with winter's purest white, as fair,
As fresh and spotless as he ever sheds
On field or mountain. Moving Form was none
Save here and there a shadowy Passenger,
Slow, shadowy, silent, dusky, and beyond
And high above this winding length of street,
This noiseless and unpeopled avenue,
Pure, silent, solemn, beautiful, was seen
The huge majestic Temple of St Paul
In awful sequestration, through a veil,
Through its own sacred veil of falling snow.

Wordsworth is full of wonder and amazement at the way St Paul's Cathedral stands majestically, alone above the streets but partly hidden by the falling snow.

'awful': awe-inspiring   *'sequestration': to be alone or hidden*

Composed upon Westminster Bridge

Earth has not any thing to show more fair:
Dull would he be of soul who could pass by
A sight so touching in its majesty:
This City now doth like a garment wear
The beauty of the morning; silent, bare,
Ships, towers, domes, theatres, and temples lie
Open unto the fields, and to the sky;
All bright and glittering in the smokeless air.
Never did sun more beautifully steep
In his first splendour valley, rock, or hill;
Ne'er saw I, never felt, a calm so deep!
The river glideth at his own sweet will:
Dear God! the very houses seem asleep;
And all that mighty heart is lying still!

Travelling

Throughout his life, William Wordsworth enjoyed the thrill of travelling and exploring new places. One of his most memorable journeys was in 1790 while he was at university. Like many modern students, he took advantage of the long holidays to go travelling and undertook a walking tour through France to Switzerland and northern Italy with a friend, Robert Jones. The following year the two of them spent the summer in North Wales.

Travelling through the Alps

The brook and road
Were fellow-travellers in this gloomy pass,
And with them did we journey several hours
At a slow step. The immeasurable height
Of woods decaying, never to be decayed,
The stationary blasts of waterfalls,
And everywhere along the hollow rent
Winds thwarting winds, bewildered and forlorn,
The torrents shooting from the clear blue sky,
The rocks that muttered close upon our ears –
Black drizzling crags that spake by the wayside
As if a voice were in them – the sick sight
And giddy prospect of the raving stream,
The unfettered clouds and region of the heavens,
Tumult and peace, the darkness and the light,
Were all like workings of one mind, the features
Of the same face, blossoms upon one tree,
Characters of the great apocalypse,
The types and symbols of eternity,
Of first, and last, and midst, and without end.

In those days, travelling through the towering mountains of the Alps was not for the faint-hearted! In this piece of poetry, the awesome forces of nature which surround Wordsworth remind him that everything on earth is connected because it is all created by God ('like workings of one mind').

'thwarting': hindering or getting in the way of something
'unfettered': not tied down, unrestrained   'tumult': noise
'apocalypse': the future of the world

Lost in the Woods

We left the town
Of Gravedona with this hope, but soon
Were lost, bewildered among woods immense,
Where, having wandered for a while, we stopped
And on a rock sat down to wait for day.
An open place it was and overlooked
From high the sullen water underneath,
On which a dull red image of the moon
Lay bedded, changing oftentimes its form
Like an uneasy snake. Long time we sat,
For scarcely more than one hour of the night –
Such was our error – had been gone when we
Renewed our journey. On the rock we lay
And wished to sleep, but could not for the stings
Of insects, which with noise like that of noon
Filled all the woods.

*Hoping to get up early to see the dawn over Lake Como in Italy,
Wordsworth and his companions get confused by the chiming of the
local church clock and find that they have actually begun their journey
in the middle of the night! Losing their way, they resign themselves to
spending the rest of the night in the woods*

The cry of unknown birds,
The mountains – more by darkness visible
And their own size, than any outward light –
The breathless wilderness of clouds, the clock
That told with unintelligible voice
The widely parted hours, the noise of streams
And sometimes rustling motions nigh at hand
Which did not leave us free from personal fear,
And lastly, the withdrawing moon that set
Before us while she still was high in heaven –
These were our food, and such a summer night
Did to that pair of golden days succeed,
With now and then a doze and snatch of sleep,
On Como's Banks, the same delicious lake.

*The night drags on with 'widely parted hours'. They all lie wide-awake
in fear of strange and unknown noises in the woods. After their terrible
night however, they are rewarded with two glorious days of lazing in the
sun by the lake.*

'unintelligible': not possible to understand   'nigh at hand': close to

Climbing Snowdon

It was a summer's night, a close warm night,
Wan, dull, and glaring, with a dripping mist
Low-hung and thick that covered all the sky,
Half threatening storm and rain; but on we went
Unchecked, being full of heart and having faith
In our tried pilot. Little could we see,
Hemmed round on every side with fog and damp,
And, after ordinary travellers' chat
With our conductor, silently we sunk
Each into commerce with his private thoughts …
When at my feet the ground appeared to brighten,
And with a step or two seemed brighter still;
Nor had I time to ask the cause of this,
For instantly a light upon the turf
Fell like a flash. I looked about, and lo,
The moon stood naked in the heavens at height
Immense above my head, and on the shore
I found myself of a huge sea of mist,
Which meek and silent rested at my feet.

One night, William Wordsworth and his friend Robert Jones climb
Snowdon, the highest mountain in Wales, with a mountain guide
(their 'pilot' or 'conductor'). As they plod upwards, each lost in their
own thoughts, the fog suddenly clears and they find themselves in the
moonlight with the cloud beneath them like a 'sea of mist'.

'wan': pale, faint

A hundred hills their dusky backs upheaved
All over this still ocean, and beyond,
Far, far beyond, the vapours shot themselves
In headlands, tongues, and promontory shapes,
Into the sea, the real sea ...
Meanwhile, the moon looked down upon this show
In single glory, and we stood, the mist
Touching our very feet; and from the shore
At distance not the third part of a mile
Was a blue chasm, a fracture in the vapour,
A deep and gloomy breathing-place, through which
Mounted the roar of waters, torrents, streams
Innumerable, roaring with one voice.

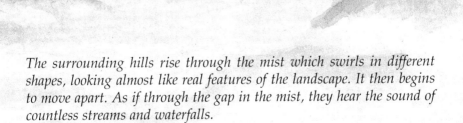

The surrounding hills rise through the mist which swirls in different shapes, looking almost like real features of the landscape. It then begins to move apart. As if through the gap in the mist, they hear the sound of countless streams and waterfalls.

'vapour': mist or cloud
'tongue', 'promontory': both mean an area of land that juts into the sea
'chasm': a vast hole, like a ravine, canyon or crevasse

I travelled among unknown Men

I travelled among unknown Men,
   In Lands beyond the Sea;
Nor England! did I know till then
   What love I bore to thee.

'Tis past, that melancholy dream!
   Nor will I quit thy shore
A second time; for still I seem
   To love thee more and more.

Among thy mountains did I feel
   The joy of my desire;
And She I cherished turned her wheel
   Beside an English fire.

Thy mornings showed – thy nights concealed
   The bowers where Lucy played;
And thine is, too, the last green field
   Which Lucy's eyes surveyed!

It seems likely that Lucy is an imaginary character, not a real person.

'melancholy': sad, depressed   'cherished': to feel affection for
'turned her wheel': a wheel for spinning wool
'bower': a shelter sometimes made from twigs and branches

Grasmere and Dove Cottage

William and Dorothy Wordsworth moved into Dove Cottage, Grasmere on 20 December 1799. William was twenty-nine years old and Dorothy celebrated her twenty-eighth birthday five days later, on Christmas day. It was a turning point in both their lives.

For Wordsworth, returning to live in his beloved Lake District provided the chance to concentrate on his poetry and find fresh inspiration. For unmarried Dorothy, it meant a permanent home and security plus the opportunity she longed for, of being able to support her brother's writing.

Grasmere is one of the Lake District's loveliest valleys. William and Dorothy immediately fell in love with it and regarded the whole valley as home. Dove Cottage, tucked away in a sheltered spot, became 'a home within a home'.

The cottage was already an old building when William and Dorothy arrived. For many years it had been an inn known as 'The Dove and Olive' so it was full of character and atmosphere. The valley, the cottage and the garden they created became major features in their lives and provided the backdrop to much of their writing.

Images of Grasmere

The Valley

Dear Valley, having in thy face a smile
Though peaceful, full of gladness. Thou art pleased,
Pleased with thy crags, and woody steeps, thy Lake,
Its one green Island and its winding shores,
The multitude of little rocky hills,
Thy Church and Cottages of mountain stone –
Clustered like stars, some few, but single most,
And lurking dimly in their shy retreats,
Or glancing at each other cheerful looks,
Like separated stars with clouds between.

A Favourite Spot

I love the fir-grove with a perfect love.
Thither do I withdraw when cloudless suns
Shine hot, or wind blows troublesome and strong;
And there I sit at evening, when the steep
Of Silver-how, and Grasmere's peaceful lake
And one green island, gleam between the stems
Of the dark firs … while o'er my head,
At every impulse of the moving breeze,
The fir-grove murmurs with a sea-like sound …

'thither': there   'grove': a small wood
'Silver-how': a hill overlooking the lake

Summer

I thought of clouds
That sail on winds; of breezes that delight
To play on water, or in endless chase
Pursue each other through the liquid depths
Of grass or corn, over and through and through,
In billow after billow, evermore;
Of Sunbeams, Shadows, Butterflies and Birds …

Winter

The birch-tree woods
Are hung with thousand thousand diamond drops
Of melted hoar-frost, every tiny knot
In the bare twigs, each little budding-place
Cased with its several bead; what myriads there
Upon one tree, while all the distant grove
That rises to the summit of the steep
Is like a mountain built of silver light …

'hoar-frost': a white frost
'myriads': countless numbers

To a Butterfly

I've watched you now a full half hour,
Self-poised upon that yellow flower;
And, little Butterfly! indeed
I know not if you sleep, or feed.
How motionless! not frozen seas
More motionless! and then
What joy awaits you, when the breeze
Hath found you out among the trees,
And calls you forth again!

This plot of Orchard-ground is ours;
My trees they are, my Sister's flowers;
Stop here whenever you are weary,
And rest as in a sanctuary!
Come often to us, fear no wrong;
Sit near us on the bough!
We'll talk of sunshine and of song;
And summer days, when we were young,
Sweet childish days, that were as long
      As twenty days are now!

'plot of Orchard-ground': Dove Cottage garden
'sanctuary': somewhere safe

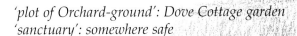

Dove Cottage Garden

Sweet Garden-orchard! of all spots that are
The loveliest surely man hath ever found.
Farewell! we leave thee to heaven's peaceful care.
Thee and the Cottage which thou dost surround …

Dear Spot! whom we have watched with tender heed,
Bringing thee chosen plants and blossoms blown
Among the distant mountains, flower and weed
Which thou hast taken to thee as thy own …

O happy Garden! loved for hours of sleep,
O quiet Garden! loved for waking hours.
For soft half-slumbers that did gently steep
Our spirits, carrying with them dreams of flowers …

These lines are from a poem written just before William and Dorothy went away for a few months.

'steep': to soak something thoroughly

from Dorothy Wordsworth's Journal …

A moment in Dove Cottage garden

6 May 1802 *A sweet morning we have put the finishing stroke to our Bower & here we are sitting in the orchard. It is one o clock. We are sitting upon a seat under the wall … It is a nice cool shady spot. The small Birds are singing – Lambs bleating, Cuckow calling – The Thrush sings by Fits, Thomas Ashburner's axe is going quietly (without passion) in the orchard – Hens are cackling, Flies humming, the women talking together at their doors – Plumb & pear trees are in Blossom, apple trees greenish – the opposite woods green, the crows are cawing. We have heard Ravens. The Ash Trees are in blossom, Birds flying all about us. The stitchwort is coming out, there is one budding Lychnis. The primroses are passing their prime. Celandine violets & wood sorrel for ever more – little geranium & pansies on the wall.*

The 'Bower' was a shelter to sit in, lined with moss
Stitchwort, lychnis, celandine and wood sorrel are wild flowers

43

A Winter Evening in Dove Cottage

What way does the Wind come? What way does he go?
He rides over the water, and over the snow,
Through wood, and through vale; and o'er rocky height,
Which the goat cannot climb, takes his sounding flight;
He tosses about in every bare tree,
As, if you look up, you plainly may see;
But how he will come, and whither he goes,
There's never a scholar in England knows ...

Hark! over the roof he makes a pause,
And growls as if he would fix his claws
Right in the slates, and with a huge rattle
Drive them down, like men in a battle:
– But let him range round; he does us no harm,
We build up the fire, we're snug and warm;
Untouched by his breath see the candle shines bright,
And burns with a clear and steady light ...

– Come now we'll to bed! and when we are there
He may work his own will, and what shall we care?
He may knock at the door, – we'll not let him in;
May drive at the windows, – we'll laugh at his din;
Let him seek his own home wherever it be;
Here's a *cozie* warm house for Edward and me.

This is from a poem written by Dorothy Wordsworth for William's three year old son John (whom she calls Edward for this poem). She imagines that the wind is like some sort of creature trying to get in the cottage. If you were to imagine the wind as a wild animal, what would you choose?

'scholar': someone with wide knowledge of a particular subject

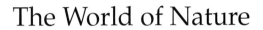

The World of Nature

Throughout his childhood, Wordsworth spent as much time outside as possible. The countryside was his playground, so it is hardly surprising that, as he grew up, he developed a deep love of the natural world. Later on, nature became one of the main subjects in his poetry. As well as describing what flowers or scenes looked like, Wordsworth liked to explore the impact that nature had on him and the way it influenced his life.

Dorothy Wordsworth, like her brother, cared passionately about her environment. Wherever she went, she was always alert to what she might see and hear, noticing every detail around her, from clouds and light effects to the tiniest flowers or leaves. In her journal she tried to capture her impressions of the landscape exactly as she experienced it.

Look out for the descriptions by Dorothy which link directly with her brother's poems: they are the entries for 15 April 1802, 25 January 1798 and 18 March 1798.

from Dorothy Wordsworth's Journal …

Daffodils

15 April 1802 *It was a threatening misty morning … The wind was furious … the Lake was rough … When we were in the woods beyond Gowbarrow park we saw a few daffodils close to the water side … as we went along there were more & yet more & at last under the boughs of the trees, we saw that there was a long belt of them along the shore … I never saw daffodils so beautiful they grew among the mossy stones about & about them, some rested their heads upon these stones as on a pillow for weariness & the rest tossed & reeled & danced & seemed as if they verily laughed with the wind that blew upon them over the Lake, they looked so gay ever glancing ever changing … There was here & there a little knot & a few stragglers a few yards higher up but they were so few as not to disturb the simplicity & unity & life of that one busy highway … Rain came on, we were wet …*

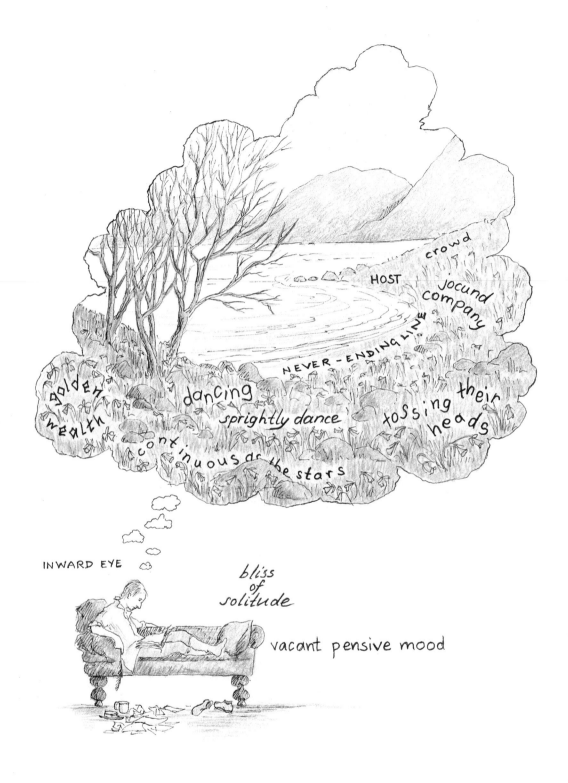

crowd

HOST

jocund company

NEVER-ENDING LINE

golden wealth

dancing

sprightly dance

tossing their heads

continuous as the stars

INWARD EYE

bliss
of
solitude

vacant pensive mood

Daffodils

I wandered lonely as a cloud
That floats on high o'er vales and hills,
When all at once I saw a crowd,
A host, of golden daffodils;
Beside the lake, beneath the trees,
Fluttering and dancing in the breeze.

Continuous as the stars that shine
And twinkle on the milky way,
They stretched in never-ending line
Along the margin of a bay:
Ten thousand saw I at a glance,
Tossing their heads in sprightly dance.

The waves beside them danced; but they
Out-did the sparkling waves in glee:
A poet could not but be gay,
In such a jocund company:
I gazed – and gazed – but little thought
What wealth the show to me had brought:

For oft, when on my couch I lie
In vacant or in pensive mood,
They flash upon that inward eye
Which is the bliss of solitude;
And then my heart with pleasure fills,
And dances with the daffodils.

'jocund': cheerful, merry
'pensive': thoughtful

To the Cuckoo

O blithe New-comer! I have heard,
I hear thee and rejoice:
O Cuckoo! shall I call thee Bird,
Or but a wandering Voice?

While I am lying on the grass,
I hear thy restless shout:
From hill to hill it seems to pass,
About, and all about!

To me, no Babbler with a tale
Of sunshine and of flowers,
Thou tellest, Cuckoo! in the vale
Of visionary hours.

Thrice welcome, Darling of the Spring!
Even yet thou art to me
No Bird; but an invisible Thing,
A voice, a mystery.

*The call of the cuckoo is instantly recognisable – but how many of us
have actually seen one? Wordsworth's unsuccessful efforts to spot a
cuckoo mean that for him, the bird's cry is far more than just a sign that
spring has arrived – it is 'no Babbler with a tale of sunshine'. It becomes
an invisible, unreal ('unsubstantial') and mysterious thing belonging
to the world of imagination. Years later it helps him to recapture the
'golden time' of his childhood.*

'blithe': merry, cheerful

The same whom in my School-boy days
I listened to; that Cry
Which made me look a thousand ways;
In bush, and tree, and sky.

To seek thee did I often rove
Through woods and on the green;
And thou wert still a hope, a love;
Still longed for, never seen!

And I can listen to thee yet;
Can lie upon the plain
And listen, till I do beget
That golden time again.

O blessed Bird! the earth we pace
Again appears to be
An unsubstantial faery place;
That is fit home for Thee!

that Cry

a mystery

a love

a wandering voice

a hope

restless shout

an invisible Thing

a voice

A Night Sky

… He looks around, the clouds are split
Asunder, and above his head he views
The clear moon and the glory of the heavens.
There in a black-blue vault she sails along
Followed by multitudes of stars, that small,
And bright, and sharp along the gloomy vault
Drive as she drives. How fast they wheel away!
Yet vanish not! The wind is in the trees;
But they are silent. Still they roll along
Immeasurably distant, and the vault
Built round by those white clouds, enormous clouds,
Still deepens its interminable depth.

The moon suddenly appears through a break in the clouds ('split asunder' means to split apart). The motion of the clouds makes it appear as if the moon and stars too are sailing swiftly through the sky, which Wordsworth imagines as a vast domed roof ('vault') over the earth.

'interminable': endless

from Dorothy Wordsworth's Journal ...

The Moon and Stars

25 January 1798 *At once the clouds seemed to
cleave asunder, and left her [the moon] in the
centre of a black-blue vault. She sailed along,
followed by multitudes of stars, small, and bright, and sharp.*

2 October 1800 *The moonlight lay upon the hills like snow.*

16 March 1802 *The Moon was a good height above the Mountains.
She seemed far & distant in the sky there were two stars beside her,
that twinkled in & out, & seemed almost like butterflies in motion &
lightness.*

31 October 1800 *The moonshine like herrings in the water.*

18 March 1802 *... the moon came out from behind a Mountain Mass of
Black Clouds – O the unutterable darkness of the sky & the Earth below
the Moon! & the glorious brightness of the moon itself! There was a vivid
sparkling streak of light at this end of Rydale water but the rest was very
dark & Loughrigg fell & Silver How were white & bright as if they were
covered with hoar frost.*

'cleave asunder': split apart
*Loughrigg fell and Silver How are hills overlooking Rydal Water and
Grasmere*

A Whirl-blast

A whirl-blast from behind the hill
Rushed o'er the wood with startling sound;
Then – all at once the air was still,
And showers of hail stones pattered round.
Where leafless oaks towered high above,
I sat within an undergrove
Of tallest hollies, tall and green;
A fairer bower was never seen.
From year to year the spacious floor
With withered leaves is covered o'er,
And all the year the bower is green.

But see! where'er the hailstones drop
The withered leaves all skip and hop;
There's not a breeze – no breath of air –
Yet here, and there, and every where
Along the floor, beneath the shade
By those embowering hollies made,
The leaves in myriads jump and spring,
As if with pipes and music rare
Some Robin Good-fellow were there,
And all those leaves, in festive glee,
Were dancing to the minstrelsy.

Walking in a wood one day in March 1798, Wordsworth is startled by a whirlwind ('whirl-blast'). The air then suddenly becomes totally still and it begins to hail. Sheltering under some holly trees, he watches as fallen leaves are hit by the hailstones.

'Robin Good-fellow': a mischievous fairy or goblin popular in old folk stories. Also known as Puck, he traditionally plays pranks and tricks on human beings, and is a character in Shakespeare's 'A Midsummer Night's Dream'.
'minstrelsy': music (a minstrel was a medieval singer and musician)

from Dorothy Wordsworth's Journal ...

The wind in the trees

18 March 1798 *... sheltered under the hollies during a hail-shower. The withered leaves danced with the hailstones. William wrote a description of the storm.*

1 February 1798 *The trees almost roared, & the ground seemed in motion with the multitudes of dancing leaves, which made a rustling sound distinct from that of the trees.*

2 April 1798 *The still trees only gently bowed their heads, as if listening to the wind.*

24 November 1801 *... our favorite Birch tree ... was yielding to the gusty wind with all its tender twigs, the sun shone upon it & it glanced in the wind like a flying sunshiny shower – it was a tree in shape with stem & branches but it was like a Spirit of water ...*

7 March 1798 *One only leaf upon the top of a tree – the sole remaining leaf – danced round and round like a rag blown by the wind.*

Storm on Coniston Water

It was a day
Upon the edge of autumn, fierce with storm;
The wind blew down the vale of Coniston
Compressed as in a tunnel; from the lake
Bodies of foam took flight, and every thing
Was wrought into commotion high and low,
A roaring wind, mist, and bewildered showers,
Ten thousand thousand waves, mountains and crags,
And darkness and the sun's tumultuous light.
Green leaves were rent in handfuls from the trees …
Meanwhile, by what strange chance I cannot tell,
What combination of the wind and clouds,
A large unmutilated rainbow stood
Immoveable in heaven.

'wrought': made   'bewildered': confused
'tumultuous': wild, stormy   'unmutilated': whole

56

from Dorothy Wordsworth's Journal ...

Stormy weather

18 March 1802 ... *the lake was covered all over with Bright silver waves that were there each the twinkling of an eye, then others rose up & took their place as fast as they went away.*

4 November 1800 ... *he (William) was obliged to lie down in the tremendous wind – the snow blew from Helvellyn horizontally like smoke ...*

5 July 1802 *The Rain met us ... & it came on very heavily afterwards. It drove past Nab Scar in a substantial shape, as if going Grasmere-wards as fast as it could go.*

29 January 1798 *A very stormy day ... Nothing distinguishable but a heavy blackness.*

29 December 1801 *As we ascended the hills it grew very cold & slippery ... A sharp hail shower gathered at the head of Martindale ... the wild cottages seen through the hurrying hail shower – the wind drove & eddied about & about & the hills looked large & swelling through the storm.*

'Nab Scar': a crag, or cliff, overlooking Rydal water
'eddied': an eddy is air or water swirling around in a circular movement

The morning after a storm

There was a roaring in the wind all night;
The rain came heavily and fell in floods;
But now the sun is rising calm and bright;
The birds are singing in the distant woods;
Over his own sweet voice the Stock-dove broods;
The Jay makes answer as the Magpie chatters;
And all the air is filled with pleasant noise of waters.

All things that love the sun are out of doors;
The sky rejoices in the morning's birth;
The grass is bright with rain-drops; on the moors
The Hare is running races in her mirth;
And with her feet she from the plashy earth
Raises a mist; which, glittering in the sun,
Runs with her all the way, wherever she doth run.

stock-dove, jay and magpie are birds
'mirth': merriment   'plashy': wet, soggy

People

In this section you will find the following poems:

'We are Seven': *Wordsworth imagines a conversation between a small child and an adult who is puzzled by the girl's attitude to the deaths of her brother and sister. Instead of grieving, she treats them as if they are still part of her daily life. The efforts of the adult to make her see reality are like 'throwing words away'. As the poem is in the form of a conversation, two voices can read it aloud. To make this easier, what the girl says has been written in italics.*

'The Sparrow's Nest': *in his poetry, Wordsworth sometimes writes about his sister Dorothy, although he often re-names her Emmeline or Emma. In this poem, finding a sparrow's nest reminds Wordsworth of how, when he and Dorothy were little, they discovered a similar nest which they looked at every day. Dorothy was torn between wanting to see the nest closely but being fearful of disturbing the baby birds. Her sensitivity is typical of the ways she has influenced him over the years.*

'Lucy Gray': *this tragic story is set on wild and lonely moorland. What happens to Lucy after she gets lost in the snow is a mystery – Wordsworth leaves the story open to our imaginations. What do you think happens? Suppose that you could ask Lucy one question, what would you ask?*

'She dwelt among the untrodden ways': *the poem tells us very little about Lucy but the images of a half-hidden violet and a single star in the sky, together with the fact that she lives 'unknown' among 'untrodden' paths, hint at a solitary life closer to the world of nature than the busy human world.*

'September 1st, 1802': *in France, Wordsworth meets a black woman who has had to flee from her home, a victim of a new law passed by the French government under Napoleon Buonaparte. Under this law, every black person in France was forced to leave the country. Wordsworth's poem reflects his anger at this unjust, heartless act.*

'The Solitary Reaper': *this poem has its origins in a tour of Scotland that William and Dorothy made in 1803. What captured Wordsworth's imagination was the fact that the girl was singing in the Scottish language, Gaelic, so he could only guess what the song might be about.*

'The Old Cumberland Beggar': *Wordsworth gives us a vivid and moving description of the old man. His body is so bent that he can only see the ground in front of his feet instead of the surrounding countryside and his progress is so slow that everyone else on the road leaves him behind.*

'To Toussaint L'Ouverture': *Toussaint L'Ouverture was the leader of black slaves on the West Indian island of Haiti, then owned by France. His efforts to achieve freedom and justice for his people resulted in his imprisonment. He died in a Paris jail. Wordsworth writes his poem as if he is talking to Toussaint L'Ouverture. He is confident that even though Toussaint himself might die, his cause will live on after his death.*

We are Seven

A simple child, dear brother Jim,
That lightly draws its breath,
And feels its life in every limb,
What should it know of death?

I met a little cottage girl,
She was eight years old, she said;
Her hair was thick with many a curl
That clustered round her head. .

She had a rustic, woodland air,
And she was wildly clad;
Her eyes were fair, and very fair,
– Her beauty made me glad.

'Sisters and brothers, little maid,
How many may you be?'
'How many? seven in all', she said,
And wondering looked at me.

'And where are they, I pray you tell?'
She answered, *'Seven are we,*
And two of us at Conway dwell,
And two are gone to sea.

Two of us in the church-yard lie,
My sister and my brother,
And in the church-yard cottage, I
Dwell near them with my mother.'

'You say that two at Conway dwell,
And two are gone to sea,
Yet you are seven; I pray you tell
Sweet Maid, how this may be?'

Then did the little Maid reply,
'Seven boys and girls are we;
Two of us in the church-yard lie,
Beneath the church-yard tree.'

'You run about, my little maid,
Your limbs they are alive;
If two are in the church-yard laid,
Then ye are only five.'

'Their graves are green, they may be seen,'
The little Maid replied,
'Twelve steps or more from my mother's door,
And they are side by side.

My stockings there I often knit,
My 'kerchief there I hem;
And there upon the ground I sit -
I sit and sing to them.

And often after sunset, Sir,
When it is light and fair,
I take my little porringer,
And eat my supper there.

The first that died was little Jane;
In bed she moaning lay,
Till God released her of her pain,
And then she went away.

So in the church-yard she was laid,
And all the summer dry,
Together round her grave we played,
My brother John and I.

And when the ground was white with snow,
And I could run and slide,
My brother John was forced to go,
And he lies by her side.'

'How many are you then,' said I,
'If they two are in Heaven?'
The little Maiden did reply,
'O Master! we are seven.'

'But they are dead; those two are dead!
Their spirits are in heaven!'
'Twas throwing words away; for still
The little Maid would have her will,
And said, *'Nay, we are seven!'*

from Dorothy Wordsworth's Journal …

Children

22 April 1802 *We saw a family of little Children sheltering themselves under a wall before the rain came on, they sate in a Row making a canopy for each other of their clothes.*

4 May 1802 *On the Rays we met a woman with 2 little girls one in her arms the other about 4 years old walking by her side, a pretty little thing, but half starved. She had on a pair of slippers that had belonged to some gentlemans child, down at the heels, but it was not easy to keep them on – but, poor thing! young as she was, she walked carefully with them. Alas too young for such cares & such travels.*

10 June 1800 *… I saw two boys before me, one about 10 the other about 8 years old at play chasing a butterfly. They were wild figures, not very ragged, but without shoes & stockings; the hat of the elder was wreathed round with yellow flowers, the younger whose hat was only a rimless crown, had stuck it round with laurel leaves. They continued at play till I drew very near & then they addressed me with the Begging cant & the whining voice of sorrow …*

16 June 1800 *We met near Skelleth a pretty little Boy with a wallet over his shoulder he came from Hawkshead & was going to 'late' a lock of meal. He spoke gently & without complaint. When I asked him if he got enough to eat he looked surprized & said 'Nay'. He was 7 years old but seemed not more than 5.*

'the Rays': Dunmail Raise, a mountain pass near Grasmere
'Begging cant': the customary way in which beggars ask for money
'late a lock of meal': beg for food

The Sparrow's Nest

Look, five blue eggs are gleaming there!
Few visions have I seen more fair,
Nor many prospects of delight
More pleasing than that simple sight!
I started, seeming to espy
The home and sheltered bed,
The Sparrow's dwelling, which, hard by
My Father's House, in wet or dry,
My Sister Emmeline and I
      Together visited.

She looked at it as if she feared it;
Still wishing, dreading to be near it:
Such heart was in her, being then
A little Prattler among men.
The Blessing of my later years
Was with me when a Boy;
She gave me eyes, she gave me ears;
And humble cares, and delicate fears;
A heart, the fountain of sweet tears;
      And love, and thought, and joy.

'started': to be taken by surprise
'espy': see, or spy something   'hard by': close to
'prattler': to 'prattle' means to chatter or babble

67

Lucy Gray

Oft had I heard of Lucy Gray,
And when I crossed the Wild,
I chanced to see at break of day
The solitary Child.

No Mate, no comrade Lucy knew;
She dwelt on a wide Moor,
The sweetest Thing that ever grew
Beside a human door!

You yet may spy the Fawn at play,
The Hare upon the Green;
But the sweet face of Lucy Gray
Will never more be seen.

'solitary': alone
'comrade': friend, companion
'fawn': a baby deer

'To-night will be a stormy night,
You to the Town must go,
And take a lantern, Child, to light
Your Mother through the snow.'

'That, Father! will I gladly do;
'Tis scarcely afternoon—
The Minster-clock has just struck two,
And yonder is the Moon.'

At this the Father raised his hook
And snapped a faggot-band;
He plied his work, and Lucy took
The lantern in her hand.

'faggot': a bundle of sticks
'plied': to carry on steadily, or persevere with something

Not blither is the mountain roe,
With many a wanton stroke
Her feet disperse the powdery snow
That rises up like smoke.

The storm came on before its time,
She wandered up and down,
And many a hill did Lucy climb
But never reached the Town.

'blither': merry, cheerful
'roe': a type of deer
'wanton': uncontrolled

The wretched Parents all that night
Went shouting far and wide;
But there was neither sound nor sight
To serve them for a guide.

At day-break on a hill they stood
That overlooked the Moor;
And thence they saw the Bridge of Wood
A furlong from their door.

And now they homeward turned, and cried
'In Heaven we all shall meet!'
When in the snow the Mother spied
The print of Lucy's feet.

'thence': from there
'furlong': an eighth of a mile

Then downward from the steep hill's edge
They tracked the footmarks small;
And through the broken hawthorn-hedge,
And by the long stone-wall;

And then an open field they crossed,
The marks were still the same;
They tracked them on, nor ever lost,
And to the Bridge they came.

They followed from the snowy bank
The footmarks, one by one,
Into the middle of the plank,
And further there were none.

Yet some maintain that to this day
She is a living Child,
That you may see sweet Lucy Gray
Upon the lonesome Wild.

O'er rough and smooth she trips along,
And never looks behind;
And sings a solitary song
That whistles in the wind.

'maintain': believe

She dwelt among the untrodden ways

She dwelt among the untrodden ways
    Beside the springs of Dove,
A Maid whom there were none to praise
    And very few to love.

A Violet by a mossy stone
    Half-hidden from the Eye!
– Fair, as a star when only one
    Is shining in the sky!

She *lived* unknown, and few could know
    When Lucy ceased to be;
But she is in her Grave, and Oh!
    The difference to me.

September 1st, 1802

We had a fellow-Passenger who came
From Calais with us, gaudy in array,
A Negro Woman like a Lady gay,
Yet silent as a woman fearing blame;
Dejected, meek, yea pitiably tame,
She sat, from notice turning not away,
But on our proffered kindness still did lay
A weight of languid speech, or at the same
Was silent, motionless in eyes and face.
She was a Negro Woman driven from France,
Rejected like all others of that race,
Not one of whom may now find footing there;
This the poor Out-cast did to us declare,
Nor murmured at the unfeeling Ordinance.

'gaudy in array': wearing brightly coloured clothes
'Ordinance': a law

The Solitary Reaper

Behold her, single in the field,
Yon solitary Highland Lass!
Reaping and singing by herself;
Stop here, or gently pass!
Alone she cuts, and binds the grain,
And sings a melancholy strain;
O listen! for the Vale profound
Is overflowing with the sound.

No Nightingale did ever chaunt
So sweetly to reposing bands
Of Travellers in some shady haunt,
Among Arabian Sands:
No sweeter voice was ever heard
In spring-time from the Cuckoo-bird,
Breaking the silence of the seas
Among the farthest Hebrides.

Will no one tell me what she sings?
Perhaps the plaintive numbers flow
For old, unhappy, far-off things,
And battles long ago:
Or is it some more humble lay,
Familiar matter of today?
Some natural sorrow, loss, or pain,
That has been, and may be again!

Whate'er the theme, the Maiden sang
As if her song could have no ending;
I saw her singing at her work,
And o'er the sickle bending;
I listened till I had my fill:
And, as I mounted up the hill,
The music in my heart I bore,
Long after it was heard no more.

'melancholy strain': a sad piece of music
'chaunt': chant or rhythmic song
'Hebrides': islands off the west coast of Scotland
'plaintive numbers': mournful, sad songs
'lay': a song

The Old Cumberland Beggar

He travels on, a solitary Man,
His age has no companion. On the ground
His eyes are turned, and, as he moves along,
They move along the ground; and evermore,
Instead of common and habitual sight
Of fields with rural works, of hill and dale,
And the blue sky, one little span of earth
Is all his prospect. Thus, from day to day,
Bowbent, his eyes for ever on the ground,
He plies his weary journey, seeing still,
And never knowing that he sees, some straw,
Some scattered leaf, or marks which, in one track,
The nails of cart or chariot wheel have left
Impressed on the white road, in the same line,
At distance still the same.

'span': an extent or distance   'prospect': a view
'plies': to carry on steadily or persevere with something

86

Poor Traveller!
His staff trails with him, scarcely do his feet
Disturb the summer dust, he is so still
In look and motion that the cottage curs,
Ere he have passed the door, will turn away
Weary of barking at him. Boys and girls,
The vacant and the busy, maids and youths,
And urchins newly breeched all pass him by:
Him even the slow-paced waggon leaves behind.

'staff': a long, wooden pole
'curs': dogs   'ere': before
'urchin': a scruffy, mischievous boy
'newly breeched': breeches are a type of trousers

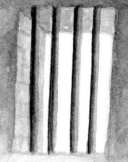

To Toussaint L'Ouverture

Toussaint, the most unhappy Man of Men!
Whether the rural Milk-maid by her Cow
Sing in thy hearing, or thou liest now
Alone in some deep dungeon's earless den,
O miserable Chieftain! where and when
Wilt thou find patience? Yet die not; do thou
Wear rather in thy bonds a cheerful brow:
Though fallen Thyself, never to rise again,
Live, and take comfort. Thou hast left behind
Powers that will work for thee; air, earth, and skies;
There's not a breathing of the common wind
That will forget thee; thou hast great allies;
Thy friends are exultations, agonies,
And love, and Man's unconquerable mind.

'bonds': chains
'exultations': to 'exult' is to rejoice

from Dorothy Wordsworth's Journal ...

Old Folk

8 February 1802 *We walked on very wet through
the clashy cold roads in bad spirits at the idea
of having to go as far as Rydale, but before we
had come again to the shore of the Lake, we met
our patient, bow-bent Friend [the letter-carrier] with his little wooden
box at his Back. 'Where are you going?' said he, 'To Rydale for letters'
– 'I have two for you in my Box.' We lifted up the Lid & there they lay
– Poor Fellow, he straddled & pushed on with all his might but we soon
out-stripped him far away when we had turned back with our letters.
We were very thankful that we had not to go on, for we should have been
sadly tired. In thinking of this I could not help comparing lots with him!
he goes at that slow pace every morning, & after having wrought a hard
days work returns at night, however weary he may be, takes it all quietly
… & has no luxury to look forward to but falling asleep in bed …*

5 March 1802 *I saw before me sitting in the open field upon his Sack of
Rags the old Ragman that I know – his coat is of Scarlet in a thousand
patches …*

3 October 1800 *… we met an old man almost double, he had on a coat
thrown over his shoulders above his waistcoat & coat. Under this he
carried a bundle & had an apron on & a night cap … his trade was to
gather leeches but now leeches are scarce & he had not strength for it –
he lived by begging & was making his way to Carlisle … He had
been hurt in driving a cart his leg broke his body driven over his skull
fractured – he felt no pain till he recovered from his first insensibility.*

10 October 1800 *The Cockermouth Traveller came with thread hardware
mustard, etc. She is very healthy, has travelled over the mountains these
thirty years. She does not mind the storms if she can keep her goods dry.*

Notes on the Poems

Many of the poems in this selection are actually extracts from longer poems. The one from which extracts are taken most frequently is *The Prelude*, which is all about Wordsworth's own life. He began it in 1799 and worked at it on and off for years. The extracts used here have been taken from the earliest 1799 version and the 1805 version which was completed at Dove Cottage.

The extracts from longer poems have been given 'new' titles to give an idea of what the poetry is about.

'Spots of Time', *Special Moments from a Lake District Childhood*

A Wild Child: from *The Two-Part Prelude*, 1799, First Part, lines 16–26

The Drowned Man: from *The Two-Part Prelude*, 1799, First Part, lines 266–279

Summer in Hawkshead: from *The Two-Part Prelude*, 1799, Second Part, lines 7–16

A Summer Day at Windermere: from *The Two-Part Prelude*, 1799, Second Part, lines 179–181, 196–214

Winter in Hawkshead: from *The Two-Part Prelude*, 1799, First Part, lines 150–185

Winter Evenings: from *The Two-Part Prelude*, 1799, First Part, lines 202–212, 225–233

The Raven's Nest: from *The Two-Part Prelude*, 1799, First Part, lines 50–55, 57–66

Owl Calls: from *The Prelude*, 1805, Book 5, lines 389–404

Waiting for Horses: from *The Two-Part Prelude*, 1799, First Part, lines 330–353

Stealing a Boat: from *The Two-Part Prelude*, 1799, First Part, lines 81–129

A Golden Store of Books: from *The Prelude*, 1805, Book 5, lines 501–515

London

Images of London:
   Traffic: from *The Prelude*, 1805, Book 7, lines 158–167
   Shops: from *The Prelude*, 1805, Book 7, lines 171–174
   Crowds: from *The Prelude*, 1805, Book 7, lines 117–120 and 595–598
   Night-time: from *The Prelude*, 1805, Book 7, lines 628–629, 631–642
St Paul's Cathedral in the snow: from *St Paul's*, lines 15–28
Composed Upon Westminster Bridge: composed 3 September 1802, published 1807

Travelling

Travelling through the Alps: from *The Prelude*, 1805, Book 6, lines 553–572
Lost in the Woods: from *The Prelude*, 1805, Book 6, lines 629–657
Climbing Snowdon: from *The Prelude*, 1805, Book 13, lines 10–19, 36–59
I travelled among unknown Men: composed 1801, published 1807

Grasmere and Dove Cottage

Images of Grasmere:
    The Valley: from *Home at Grasmere*, lines 135–144
    A Favourite Spot: from *Poems on the Naming of Places VI*, lines 87–93 and
      102–104
    Summer: from *Home at Grasmere*, lines 25–31
    Winter: from *Home at Grasmere*, lines 784–791
    To a Butterfly: composed 20 April, 1802, published 1807
    Dove Cottage Garden: from *A Farewell*, composed 1802, published 1815,
      lines 5–8, 33–36 and 57–60
A Winter Evening in Dove Cottage: from *Address to a Child during a boisterous winter evening*, composed by Dorothy Wordsworth, 1806, published 1815, lines 1–8, 28–35, 38–43

The World of Nature

To the Cuckoo: composed March 23–26, 1802, published 1807
A Night Sky: from *A Night-Piece,* composed January 1798, published 1815, lines 8–19
Daffodils: Wordsworth did not give this poem a title, so it is often known by its first line, 'I wandered lonely as a cloud', composed 1804, published 1807
A Whirl-blast: as above, this poem is generally known by its first line, 'A whirl-blast from behind the hill', composed 18 March 1798, published 1800
Storm on Coniston Water: from some lines written for *The Prelude* but not used in any version
The Morning after a Storm: from *Resolution and Independence*, composed May–July 1802, published 1807, lines 1–14

People

We are Seven: composed 1798, published 1798

The Sparrow's Nest: composed 1801, published 1807

Lucy Gray: composed 1799, published 1800

She dwelt among the untrodden ways: originally titled *Song*, it is nowadays more usually known by its first line, 'She dwelt among the untrodden ways', composed 1799, published 1800

September 1st, 1802: composed 1 September 1802, published 11 February 1803 (Morning Post); 1807

The Solitary Reaper: composed November 1805, published 1807

The Old Cumberland Beggar: from a poem of the same name, composed 1797, published 1800, 44–66

To Toussaint L'Ouverture: composed August 1802, published 2 February 1803 (Morning Post); 1807